Walker Evans

Photographer of America

Walker Evans

Photographer of America

Thomas Nau

A Neal Porter Book   Roaring Brook Press   New Milford, Connecticut

Sidewalk scene, Alabama

Contents

Coney Island, New York City

Prologue
A Couple at Coney Island, New York City

1928

"I was photographing against the style of the time, against salon photography, against beauty photography, against art photography."

"I was against the grain."

Click.

A young man has aimed his small camera at a couple on the Coney Island boardwalk. They are out on a clear Sunday afternoon, enjoying the rides and the ocean breeze, looking across the water at one of Luna Park's towers. Perhaps they have taken a ride on the Thunderbolt roller coaster or the Wonder Wheel. Walker Evans, then in his late twenties, has gone to photograph the people, the rides, and the fantastic buildings that made Coney Island famous as a place of entertainment all over the world. He stares, noticing the woman's dress. He pries, paying attention to the casual elegance of the man's clothes. He takes pictures, not of wealthy ladies posing for the camera in front of a painted backdrop, like salon photographers of the day. He does not take pictures of clouds or rain-soaked trees like the art photographers, nor does he take pictures of cigarettes artfully arranged to be used for an advertisement in the newspaper. He has rejected all of these styles. Walker wants to photograph the everyday life he sees around him. With the encouragement of friends, Walker Evans is taking his first steps to becoming one of the master American photographers of the twentieth century.

Wonder Wheel at Coney Island

1

A Child of the Midwest

1903–1922

*"I'm really spiritually at home in this country. . . .
this is the essence of what's gone to make me. I respond to it."*

Walker Evans III was born on November 3, 1903, in Saint Louis, Missouri. His father, Walker Jr., was a third-generation Missourian whose ancestors had been among the earliest merchants and tradespeople settling in the state. The family of Walker's mother, Jessie, had recently come to Missouri from Michigan. Although he could count a relative who had fought in the American Revolution, both Walker Jr. and Jessie were from modest economic backgrounds. Walker Jr. had dreamed of designing houses, but his family could not afford architecture school. Instead, he entered a career in advertising, an occupation that was just developing in the first years of the twentieth century. He began his career writing ads to persuade people to purchase an item or simply listing an item for sale and its price in the newspaper. By the time his son Walker III was born, he was a vice president in a Saint Louis advertising agency. Young Walker grew up loving words and even the look and shape of letters. His lifelong attraction to signs and lettering perhaps began as a boy, thanks to his copywriter father.

In 1908, when Walker III was five years old, his father took a job in a large agency in Chicago, Illinois, and his family moved to the small suburb of Kenilworth. Walker later described Kenilworth as "very restricted, all the same kind of people . . . I didn't know it but I was only seeing privileged people with a certain amount of money and security. It was a sort of *Babes in Toyland* fairyland."

Walker Evans as a boy around 1911

Walker's lasting love of literature began in Kenilworth. At age sixty-eight he could still remember the name of the young woman who had introduced him to the excitement of books. Mrs. Phelps would read to the neighborhood children after school. "[S]he was great. With love . . . of people and children . . . and knowledge and love of literature she just opened us up to it without our knowing it." This introduction to books was vital to the art he would later make. He described his photographs as prose. Each picture, filled with the rich details of everyday life, contained a small story in itself. Several photos in sequence, looked at carefully and receptively, can be thought of as a photographic version of a small novel. "Fine photography is literature, and it should be," he would say.

In 1914 a new job opportunity for his father led to another move. Walker was eleven when the family left the "fairyland" suburb for the city of Toledo, Ohio. Walker was shocked by the contrast between the two places. While Kenilworth was overwhelmingly white and middle class, a train ride away from the ethnic, racial, and economic diversity of Chicago, Toledo was a small industrial city teeming with immigrants seeking work in the factories. Italians from southern Europe mingled with African Americans from the South and Poles and Jews from Central Europe. The move to Toledo was difficult for Walker. "I had a hard time, a rude time," he said. Perhaps Walker's sense of security had been shattered. A privileged young boy with a servant living in an enclosed middle-class community became an adolescent living in a racially, socially, and economically diverse city. Another shock came as his parents' marriage began to dissolve. When his mother and sister moved to New York City alone in January 1919, Walker was sent to Loomis, a boarding school in Connecticut. The Evans family was now scattered.

Walker changed schools several times. For one term he attended a New York City public school, and then went back to private schools, finally graduating from Phillips Academy in 1922. He had hoped to go to Yale with his upper-class friends, but was not admitted. He applied to Williams College and was accepted. Walker did not really care for school. But he had a great love of reading, sparked by Mrs. Phelps years before. Walker spent only one year at Williams and skipped most of his classes. He spent much of that time in the school library reading authors who were writing the most exciting fiction of the day: D. H. Lawrence, Virginia Woolf, and James Joyce, among others. They found the smallest details of daily life interesting and worth writing about. And they rejected the late-nineteenth-century idea that some subjects should not be discussed in "proper" society.

Walker was excited. He too wanted to honestly depict life as he saw it. He too wanted to become a writer.

2

New York–Paris–New York

1923–1928

*"I had a passion for photography. I could think about
nothing else much; reading and photography."*

After his year at Williams, Walker decided that his formal schooling was over and he
headed to New York City. The main branch of the New York Public Library, a grand
building guarded over by two huge sculptured lions at the sidewalk entrance to the
stairway, held a powerful attraction for the young man. "I was drawn to it . . . I really went
to work there because I wanted to see the stacks [of books]. . . . I went to the head of the
Library and said 'I'll work here for nothing.'" He got a job in the map room delivering
requested materials.

Walker also met a friend with whom he could discuss art and writing. Hanns Skolle
was a German painter the same age as Walker. From the time they met in the middle
1920s, Hanns and Walker supported each other's artistic efforts. Walker would admire
Hanns's paintings and woodcuts. Hanns would comment upon and praise Walker's
short stories. And when Walker began to take photographs, Hanns always had a good
word to say about them.

In the fall of 1925, Walker quit his library job, and the following spring he took the
steamship *Cherbourg* to France. He was heading to Paris, the destination for so many

12

*Hanns Skolle with
photo enlarger
by Walker Evans*

artistic young people of the time. In Paris, he vowed, he would finally become a writer. Along with his other belongings he brought a six-dollar vest-pocket camera that his father had given him. With this camera he took his first photographs. He later dismissed most of this early work—mainly portraits of himself and friends. But he also made pictures of street scenes with passersby, which hint that he already had developed an interest in photographing everyday life.

Walker enrolled at the Sorbonne to study French language and literature and between classes wrote short stories. He also translated the works of nineteenth-century French writers whom he admired, such as the prose poems of Charles Baudelaire, whose outsider spirit and insistence that artists should show the times in which they lived rather than mimic the art of the past appealed to Walker. He read Gustave Flaubert, who had included in his novels detailed descriptions of the clothes people wore, the houses they lived in, their entertainments, and the newspapers and books they read. It was an exciting time for Walker but also a time of despair. He confessed in a letter to his friend Hanns that he had burned some of the stories he had written. And Walker was a shy young man. When the owner of a bookstore offered to introduce him to his idol, James Joyce, Walker refused. "I was scared to death to meet him. I wouldn't do it. He came in and I left the shop."

Walker returned to America in May 1927. He had spent one year in France, observing and absorbing European culture. The way Europeans lived had impressed him. He learned one thing in France that served him well as a photographer. "I remember my first experience as a café sitter in Europe. *There* is a staring that startles the American.... The European. . . is *really* interested in just ordinary people and makes a study of man with his eyes in public. What a pleasure and an art it was to study back." It's possible that Walker's later interest in taking photographs of ordinary people in public places began with his pleasure at sitting in the cafés of Europe just watching the people around him.

Still intent on becoming a writer, Walker returned to New York City. He found various odd jobs while he continued to write and photograph. In rebellion against his father's middle-class aspirations, Walker did *not* want to find an "occupation." His real interest was in reading, writing, and, increasingly, in photography. He loved exploring the city, taking along the Kodak Tourist camera that his father bought him.

By 1928 Walker was living in an apartment overlooking the Brooklyn Bridge. The neighborhood in Brooklyn was filled with young writers and artists. They socialized, talked, and showed one another their work. He became friendly with the poet Hart Crane, who was working on a book-length poem about the great bridge. Walker showed Hart the pictures he had taken of it, and Hart loved them. Soon Hart was showing his friends the pictures as well as other photographs Walker had taken of the city. Another Brooklyn neighbor was Ben Shahn, who in time became a well-known painter and illustrator. Shahn was born in Lithuania and grew up in the Jewish community in the Lower East Side of New York. His art was often inspired by his upbringing and his left-wing politics. He and Walker soon began taking pictures together on the streets of the

Hart Crane by Walker Evans   *Ben Shahn*

city. Walker loved Ben's artwork, which was often based on the photos he had taken of New York City street scenes or from newspaper photographs of current events. Ben fascinated Walker. "I knew I was getting educated. After all, a little boy from Kenilworth had never seen anybody like that, the son of a Russian immigrant really right out of the streets, you know, and tough. All the things I thought were exotic and fascinating." Over the next few years Walker and Ben shared darkroom studios and for a while Walker lived in the basement below the Shahn family apartment after they had moved to Manhattan.

Walker also met another young photographer, Berenice Abbott. Although they had been in Paris at the same time they did not meet there, but rather through mutual friends in New York. Berenice had studied photography with the painter and photographer Man Ray and had taken many portraits of writers in Paris, including Walker's idol James Joyce. She had also met an aging and not widely known French photographer whose work influenced both Berenice and Walker. Eugène Atget had been a sailor and an actor before turning to photography at the age of forty-two. Atget was in love with Paris, not only the grand churches and famous monuments but also the ordinary streets and storefronts. He had been photographing Paris since 1899, and in twenty-eight years seemed to have photographed everything. When Berenice met him he was living on bread, milk, and sugar, selling his prints for artists to paint from, and to the

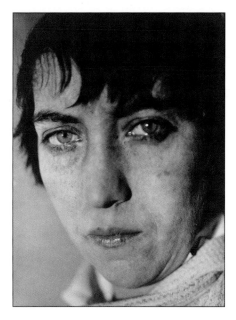

Berenice Abbott by Walker Evans

government as documentation of the city. Berenice felt she had met a genius, and when Atget died a few months after they were introduced, she took it upon herself to buy as many of the prints and glass plate negatives as she could afford—more than a thousand negatives and seven thousand prints. Berenice showed Walker some of Atget's prints, and Walker was bowled over. They showed him how beautiful and filled with poetry photographs could be. Atget's pictures gave Walker a sense that he was on the right track in photographing the streets and buildings and people around him.

At this time Walker also meet Lincoln Kirstein, who would do much to help promote Walker's career. Lincoln, the son of a wealthy Boston family, was in his early twenties but was already accomplished in many areas. At Harvard he had started the journal *Hound & Horn* to publish the latest in literature and art. Later he would found the New York City Ballet. Walker later said: "He invaded you; you either had to throw him out or listen to him ... Oddly enough, what happened was that this undergraduate was *teaching* me something about what I was doing." Lincoln also knew many people in the artistic and literary world and took Walker with him to parties and other gatherings, always touting Walker's growing body of photographic work.

Hanns, Hart, Ben, Berenice, Lincoln. An ever-growing network of friends and acquaintances fed Walker's imagination and supported his work.

Lincoln Kirstein by Walker Evans

Storefront in Paris, by Eugène Atget

Brooklyn Bridge

3
Collecting Images

1929–1935

"The secret of photography is, the camera takes on the character and the personality of the handler."

More and more, Walker was thinking of himself as an aspiring photographer rather than a budding writer. When the light was right it was hard to keep him indoors. He wanted to be out in the streets with his camera. He knew what he did not like: the sentimental, the romantic, the obviously beautiful, the commercial. What he wanted was the straightforward snapshot filled with the detail of life. But he wondered: Is this any good? Is this work too plain to be art?

And he continued his walking and picture taking throughout the city.

Click.

On Forty-second Street, he caught a woman in a fur stole. Look closely, notice the plush quality of the fur, the stylish hat . . . and look more, at the advertising lettering on the stairs of the El.

Click.

He catches workmen unloading huge lettering from a truck. In the middle of the metropolis, a sign boldly declaring a loss . . . of what? He smiles at the wit of it.

42nd Street, New York City

Damaged sign, New York City

Lunchroom buddies, New York City

Click.

In Lower Manhattan he found a short-order cook taking a break with a buddy. Are they looking forward to a night on the town?

By 1930, at the age of twenty-seven, Walker announced to a friend that he was a professional photographer. He wrote, "I am going to publish some [p]hotographs in oreder [*sic*] to become known and make someone exhibit me and sell prints and make money and take leave of [a] certain malaise." He told his friends that he was willing to do advertising work to support his creative efforts. Walker did a couple of advertising jobs but refused to do more work in that field. "After all, my father was in the advertising business. I knew what it was like. I didn't want to be like that."

Walker's photographs begin to appear in the small magazines *Architectural Review, Creative Art,* and Kirstein's *Hound & Horn.* His photos were shown in group shows in one gallery, then another. In 1930 Hart Crane's *The Bridge* was published with three of Walker's photographs. Lincoln helped organize a small show of Walker's pictures at the Harvard Society of Contemporary Art. He was included with other photographers in a show in Munich, Germany, and at a show of international photography at the Brooklyn Museum. He was becoming known in a slowly widening circle of people.

Lincoln Kirstein asked Walker to become the photographer for a project to

Walker with his view camera

document nineteenth-century American domestic architecture. They, along with John Wheelwright, a poet and architect from a wealthy Boston family, would climb in a Ford Model T, with Walker in the rumble seat, and explore small towns in New England. Lincoln recalled how Walker was sometimes maddeningly particular about getting the perfect photograph. He always wanted to work when the light was directly on each house and did not want shadows falling onto it. He would slowly set up his large camera on a tripod, put his head under the black cloth, and carefully frame the desired image, then adjust the camera and lens.

Maine pump

Click. He had captured all the details of the house.

In the winter of 1932, Walker was given what seemed like a great assignment. Through Hart Crane he became the photographer on a yacht sailing to the South Pacific. On New Year's Day the boat set sail on a four-month journey to Tahiti. He found that being on the open sea for a month at a time with only the horizon to look at was boring. Walker's work from this job seems to reflect his lack of interest in the voyage and the guests, whom he tended to view as spoiled rich people. He shot movie footage—one of the very few times he did this in his career—as well as still pictures of guests, the crew, the South Sea natives, and the islands. He managed to climb the rigging of the ship to make photographs—despite his fear of heights. Although Walker never joined a political party or committed to a political group, he was moved by the ill treatment of the natives by the French colonial administrators and found the decline of their culture "too painful and infuriating to look at for long."

In 1933 his friend Ernestine Evans, an editor at a publishing house, helped arrange a job for Walker making pictures for a book on Cuba by Carleton Beals. *The Crime of Cuba* was about the Cuban dictator Gerardo Machado and those opposing him. Always independent even when he needed the money, Walker did not want to be told what to photograph but wanted to be left alone to seek his own subjects. In fact, he didn't even read the book! Armed with letters of introduction to reporters and an array of cameras, he sailed for Cuba. His pictures from those three weeks in Cuba tell a story about the way the people there lived.

Click.

Caught unawares, a smartly dressed man in white suit and straw boater hat surveys his domain. The Coca-Cola sign and movie magazines are American products that have become a part of the Cuban landscape as well.

Citizen in Downtown Havana

Coal loader, Havana

Click.

Covered in soot and dirt, with his shovel over his shoulder and the remains of a hat, a gray beard framing his lower face, this stevedore looks a bit stern but not unkind.

26

Shoeshine stand detail, southeastern U.S.

While money was always in short supply, Walker was getting small jobs here and there. He photographed artwork for private galleries and received a job photographing African sculpture for the Metropolitan Museum of Art. He also photographed the houses of wealthy acquaintances. In 1935 he was hired by the carpet manufacturer and theatrical producer Gifford Cochran to photograph the plantations of the South. As with Lincoln, Cochran loved old American architecture and wanted to alert people to its beauty and the need to preserve it. A book with great pictures would help. In February Walker hopped into a chauffeured sedan with Gifford and headed south. He took along a small 35mm camera, a four-by-five-inch Speed Graphic, and an

Jane Ninas by Walker Evans

eight-by-ten-inch view camera. Walker made some memorable images along the way. He photographed houses, streets, stores, and signs in Savannah, Georgia. Gifford and Walker spent some time in Atlanta, and then proceeded to New Orleans.

Walker loved New Orleans. It was a city filled with fanciful houses plastered and painted in vivid reds, pinks, blues, and greens and decorated with grillwork and gingerbread. And he found another reason to like New Orleans when he met Jane Smith Ninas. Walker was immediately and deeply attracted to Jane. She had come to New Orleans as a college student to study art and had met and married another artist, Paul Ninas. By the time Walker arrived, Jane and Paul's marriage was in trouble, and Paul was seeing another woman. With Paul caught up in his own affairs Jane was often alone, and Walker would ask her to accompany him on his photographic expeditions. Together they explored the Belle Grove Plantation, where Walker photographed the entire house, details of the columns, and the window decoration. Then he went inside and set up his large camera on its tripod.

Click.

He caught the walls of a huge dining hall ringed with stately columns, now empty and slowly falling into disrepair. What magnificent dining parties had taken place here? And what had happened to the society who built these huge houses and then were forced to let them go?

Soon Walker had to leave New Orleans, but he didn't forget Jane. He wrote to her asking if she would come visit him in New York. They began seeing each other when they could. Jane would come up to New York or go with Walker on his photo assignments, sketching while he photographed.

This was a time of economic uncertainty. With the stock market crash of 1929, the economy had been shattered. Companies closed down. One in every three American workers was without a job. In the 1932 presidential race, Franklin D. Roosevelt defeated President Herbert Hoover with a promise that he would reform the government and improve the economy. With the help of Congress, the new president began an ambitious series of programs to get the economy—and the people—working again. Roosevelt had an idea to get artists and writers working, too. As part of the Works Progress Administration, a newly created government agency, writers would be hired to create guides to all the cities and states; painters would make murals in airports, libraries, government buildings, and post offices throughout the land. And photographers would be hired to document people living in economic hardship and the positive effects of the

Breakfast room at Belle Grove Plantation

new social programs. Some of the best photographers of the time worked in the WPA: Dorothea Lange, Jack Delano, Russell Lee, Marian Post Wolcott, and Walker's friend Ben Shahn. Once again Ernestine Evans helped out, urging the people she knew in government to hire Walker for the newly created Resettlement Administration, an agency devoted to building new housing. In 1935 Walker was hired to photograph examples of both run-down homes and the new government-funded housing. He considered this the perfect job. He was being paid a steady salary to do his own work and was given the photographic supplies he needed. As usual, he mostly refused to follow the assignments, instead photographing the people and places that attracted him. It allowed him, he later said, "[to develop] my own eye, my own feeling about this country. . . . that was great for me!"

And he always followed his principles: His photography "is pure record not propaganda. . . . NO POLITICS whatever."

A list of some of the places he visited while working for the Resettlement Administration shows how much he traveled: Pittsburgh, Pennsylvania, and vicinity; the Ohio Valley and Cincinnati, Ohio; Nashville, Tennessee; Vicksburg and Natchez, Mississippi; Savannah and Atlanta, Georgia; New Orleans, Louisiana; Beaufort and Columbus, South Carolina.

Walker Evans in the 1930s

Houses, Atlanta, Georgia

Click.

Looking at two frame houses in Atlanta with billboards advertising the latest movies, an increasingly new sight in America.

Joe's Auto Graveyard, Easton, Pennsylvania

Click.

He noticed the beginnings of another new American landscape in Joe's Auto Graveyard.

Click.

And throughout his travels he took pictures of people, at an American Legionnaire's parade...

American Legionnaire

Street scene, Kingwood, West Virginia

…or simply hanging out on small-town and city streets.

Floyd Burroughs with Tengle children

4

Three Tenant Families

1936

"I don't think an artist is directly able to alleviate the human condition. He's very interested in revealing it."

Nineteen thirty-six was a good year for Walker. He was traveling the eastern and southern United States making photographs in his own style and with a government salary. In the summer Walker's friend James Agee presented him with one of the greatest opportunities of his career, the chance to photograph tenant farmers in their homes and fields.

James Agee was one of several remarkable American writers and poets who worked for the business magazine *Fortune* in the 1930s and '40s. At twenty-seven, tall, gangly, and given to wearing inexpensive clothes so as to deny any sense of social superiority, James was also a nonstop talker. More than one person reported that Agee, fueled by liquor and cigarettes, would keep them up until three or four in the morning talking. He was also a very gifted writer who would go on to write distinguished film criticism and win the Pulitzer Prize for his novel *A Death in the Family*. Walker had met James a couple of years earlier, and discovered that they shared an intense interest in indigenous American culture—the style found in common homes and clothes and the everyday speech, songs, and entertainments of ordinary people.

When Agee was given an opportunity to write an article on tenant farmers for *Fortune* magazine, he urged the editor to hire Walker as the photographer. Walker was excited by the offer. He respected Agee's talent, and having photographed in the South he knew this would be an excellent opportunity. Walker also knew that Jim, who projected both empathy and a friendly manner, and who was from Tennessee, would have an easier time making contacts with white southerners.

Walker went to his boss in the Resettlement Administration, Roy Stryker, and asked for a leave of absence to work on the story. It was an assignment that would appeal to the government. Farmers had been among the hardest hit by the depression, and tenant farmers, or sharecroppers, were the poorest of the agricultural workers. After the Civil War, tenancy had replaced slavery as the major labor system in the South, the difference being that tenants could leave. The tenant farm family did not own its home or the farm it worked, and often it did not own its own farm tools or mules. The family worked the landowner's farm and in exchange for its shelter and a means to feed itself, the tenant paid a portion of the year's crop to the landowner. This portion was from one-half down to one-quarter of the crop. At times the landlord would provide money for seed, fertilizer, doctor bills, and other expenses. Whatever money the tenant farmers made from their portion of the harvest would be paid back to the landlord for the loaned money, plus extra money as interest. As a result the tenant family was often in constant debt.

Stryker liked the idea of documenting a tenant family, and made a deal with *Fortune*. Walker would be given a leave of absence without pay from his government work. *Fortune* would pay all photographic, traveling, and living expenses in exchange for the right to first publish Walker's photographs with James Agee's story in the magazine. After that, the publishing rights would belong to the U. S. government.

James Agee by Walker Evans

By July, Walker and James were heading down to Alabama in their car. They spent three weeks traveling along the county dirt roads looking for a "typical" tenant farm family. The magazine had not provided any good leads. Then one day while standing outside the county courthouse of Greensboro, Alabama, Walker began a conversation with Frank Tengle, whom Agee later called Fred Ricketts when he wrote about this experience. Tengle was in town with his brother-in-law Bud Fields and Fields's son-in-law Floyd Burroughs in the hope of finding temporary government work. Walker had found his subjects. The sharecroppers probably thought that since Walker worked for the Resettlement Administration he could help them out. And in a small way, he could. The three families agreed to put up James and Walker in the Burroughs home. In exchange, James and Walker would provide the families much needed income.

Burroughs home

The local citizens of the Alabama county had clear opinions of the three families.

"Frank Ricketts [Tengle]? Why, that dirty son-of-a-bitch, he brags *that he hasn't bought his family a bar of soap in five year."*

"None of these people has any sense, nor any initiative. If they did, they wouldn't be farming on shares."

"Give them money and all they'll do with it is throw it away."

Agee reported the simple facts of their lives: Floyd and Allie Mae Burroughs and their four children did not own the most important farm tools or the mule needed to pull the plows and wagons. Frank Tengle, who had been fortunate enough to own mules and cows, had watched his mules fall sick and die one by one. He had to sell his cows to pay debts. He fell ill with appendicitis and congestive chills and Mrs. Tengle contracted pellagra, an often fatal disease caused by poor diet. A number of their children died. The debts mounted.

Cotton farming was a difficult way to make a living. The yearly growing cycle began in late February with the plowing of the soil. Then came the planting and fertilizing. The farmer had to fight the enemies of the cotton: weeds, the army worm, the devastating insect called the boll weevil, droughts, and floods. In late summer the cotton was ready to be picked and everyone in the family helped, including all but the youngest children. Ten-year-old Louise Burroughs picked a hundred and fifty pounds of cotton a day.

It was into these lives that Walker and James entered for four weeks in the summer of 1936. They slept on thin cotton bedding on the porch, scratching furiously at bed bugs and lice. For a while they took turns sleeping in the backseat of their car. James stayed on, wanting to fully participate in the lives of those he was documenting. Walker retreated to a local hotel but returned during the day.

Burroughs fireplace

Click.

He photographed their fireplaces and living rooms...

Burroughs kitchen

Click.

…and their kitchens.

Louise Burroughs picking cottom

He photographed Louise picking cotton in late summer. And he made the photograph of Louise, dignified and shy. She wears the hat that protects her from the strong Alabama sun when she picks cotton, and she stands against the weather-whitened pine boards that are the walls of her home. How different from salon portraits, with painted backgrounds and expensive gowns! How different from the portraits of the celebrities that adorned most magazine covers! This was not photography meant to try to lure you into buying something. It was, as Walker said, the simple revealing of one young person who lived on a tenant farm in 1936 Alabama. Interestingly, it is known today, more than sixty years later, as the jacket image from Karen Hesse's novel *Out of the Dust*, winner of the Newbery Medal.

At the end of August, Walker and James packed up their car and took leave of the three tenant families they had come to like and respect. Walker set about developing the film and printing the photographs. He made a scrapbook, carefully ordering the pictures to form the story he wanted to tell. Meanwhile, James was working on the article for *Fortune*, which he submitted in early fall 1936. It was many times too long for a

Louise Burroughs

magazine article and did not present the situation from the conservative perspective of a business periodical. Dwight Macdonald, a former editor of *Fortune* and himself an important American writer, said he thought the article was "pessimistic, unconstructive, impractical, indignant, lyrical and always personal." Walker believed that Agee did not want the article printed in the magazine, and that he made sure the writing was unacceptable. Having succeeded in avoiding publication in *Fortune*, Agee hoped to publish the text and photographs as a book. Uncertain about whether his words could do justice to the full truth of the tenants' lives, he began to write and rewrite the text. It would not be published until five years later.

South Carolina

5

Recognition

1937–1941

"It's as though there's a wonderful secret in a certain place and I can capture it. Only I can do it at this moment, only this moment and only me."

Walker knew that Alabama had been very important in his growth as an artist. He had been allowed to explore a subject in detail with his cameras, much as the writers he admired had done with their pens. Now he had to go back to his government assignments. He had spent two years photographing mostly the subjects that interested him and by and large avoiding those he was assigned. "I would ignore bureaucratic orders, administration orders. . . . I wasn't going to serve anybody in this position except myself." Roy Stryker had pleaded with him to take at least some pictures that were requested, but he resisted. In 1937, when Stryker had to lay off someone owing to lack of funds, he regretfully chose Walker. Walker was again without a steady income or money for photographic supplies.

But within a year, in 1938, at the age of thirty-five, Walker received the high honor of being the first photographer to have a one-person show at the Museum of Modern Art in New York. His book, *American Photographs,* was published the same year and is generally recognized as one of the classic books of photography. The exhibition included the early photographs from Coney Island and New England. Also shown were those taken in Cuba and New Orleans as well as photographs shot when Walker was working for the Resettlement Administration. The show was praised by many for its honesty. Carl Van Vechten, an important chronicler of the literary and art movements of the time, wrote in the *New York Herald Tribune* that "as documentary evidence . . . these pictures are valuable. But I place on them a much higher value than that, the value that lies in fine photography." Others, like the reviewer in the *Washington Post*, thought it "a parade of dreary, drab, and depressing scenes." But for Walker, the positive response confirmed his act of faith in his straightforward snapshot approach. He had asked himself for years whether his work was too plain to be art. After the museum show he wondered less.

Back in New York City, Walker became excited by a new project. He planned to photograph people whom he "collected with his eyes" on the New York subway. And he wanted to photograph them without their being aware they were having their picture taken. "That's my idea of what a portrait ought to be, anonymous and documentary and a straightforward picture of mankind, not of a celebrity, not journalism." He took on the project purely for the love of it, without the promise of a paycheck. And in the winter of 1938, riding the subway with a younger photographer, Helen Levitt, he began to photograph. He concealed his small 35 mm camera within his heavy winter coat so that no one would suspect his picture taking. He and Helen seemed just like all the other subway passengers.

Click.

A messenger boy with his eyes focused on something above the passengers opposite him, wearing his uniform cap pushed back from his neatly combed hair.

Click.

A couple no longer young but not yet old, the woman wrapped in a fur-trimmed coat and the man in a black leather jacket. Is she a secretary, wanting to look good for a job interview? And does he want to look like some tough guy out of the movies?

Messenger boy in subway

Couple in subway

About the subway riders he would write, "you don't see among them the face of a judge or a senator or a bank president." He did find humor, tenderness, and loneliness. It was not until 1966, twenty-eight years later, that Walker's subway portraits were first exhibited at the Museum of Modern Art and published in book form as *Many Are Called.* In 2004 the book was republished on the one hundredth anniversary of the New York City subway system.

Walker continued to court Jane. He had placed her initials "J.N.S." on the dedication page of *American Photographs*. Walker urged her to leave her unfaithful husband and move in with him. At one point during Jane's visit to New York in the summer of 1939, Walker wrapped some of her hair around his finger and said, "With this hair I thee wed." Eventually Jane moved into Walker's small Upper East Side apartment in Manhattan with her paints and sketch pads.

In 1940 Walker was awarded a Guggenheim Foundation grant. The foundation gives one year's allotment of money to worthy people in art, music, writing, dance, science, philosophy, and other creative but poor-paying occupations. Walker had not had a steady income since working for the Resettlement Administration three years before. Now he could buy photographic supplies and support himself without worry. He planned to return to the South with Jane to continue his exploration of the people and buildings of that region. But he had an attack of appendicitis, and then caught pneumonia. His Guggenheim grant did pay off some debts, but he did little work during 1940.

In 1941 the project on tenant farmers finally became a book. James Agee had spent the years since 1936 working and reworking the text. One publishing house backed out after Agee refused to make major text changes. Another house agreed when James had made small revisions. Walker had his own battles with the publisher. One of the images in the book was a photograph of the Burroughs bedroom, the bed dotted with flies. During the preparation of the photo for printing, the flies were removed from the image. When Walker saw the test proof, he demanded that the flies be shown in the final printing. *Let Us Now Praise Famous Men* (*with* flies) was published, but it was not well received. Most newspaper and magazine reviewers liked Walker's pictures but were critical of Agee's writing. The *New York Times* reviewer wrote, "There never was a better argument for photography. . . . Mr. Evans says as much about tenant farmers . . . in his several dozen pictures as Mr. Agee says in his entire 150,000 words . . ." The literary critic Lionel Trilling, on the other hand, wrote in the *Kenyon Review* that it was "the most realistic and the most important moral effort of our American generation." The first printing sold only about six hundred copies. Yet the book was read, recommended, and read by others. *Let Us Now Praise Famous Men,* considered by some to be a classic of American social reporting, continues to be read to this day.

Though his Guggenheim year was not productive and *Let Us Now Praise Famous Men* sold few copies, at least Walker had Jane, who had recently divorced Paul Ninas. When Walker was sent to Florida on a job, Jane went with him. On their way there, they married. And the Florida trip was their honeymoon. Jane would sketch, Walker would photograph, and they would both enjoy the warmth of the late fall sunshine. As always, Walker photographed how people lived, with insight and wit.

Click.

The old gentleman sits on the tiny porch in a mobile home community. Was this the man's small patch of the American Dream?

Municipal Trailer Camp, Sarasota, Florida

6

Fortune?

1942–1964

*"With a camera, it's all or nothing. You either get what you're
after at once, or what you do has to be worthless."*

When the United States entered World War II in 1941, America changed from a country focused on economic hardship to a country focused on war. As the war effort geared up, there was a shortage of the photographic supplies Walker would need for his work, and gasoline became scarce, making it more difficult for him to travel in search of subjects. He was not photographing as much, perhaps for these reasons and perhaps because he was unsure of his next project after coming off a very creative period that spanned fourteen years.

Wanting to contribute to the war effort, he offered his services to Edward Steichen, the famous photographer who had become head of the army photographic division. He later found out that Roy Stryker had warned Steichen against hiring him. "Evans is too difficult to work with," Stryker had told Steichen. And so Walker did not get the job.

Time magazine did hire Walker to write movie and art reviews. He was finally being paid to write, although something very different from the experimental short stories of his youth. But it was good to have a steady income.

When the war ended in 1945, America entered a period of prosperity. Businesses began to thrive. More and more people were back at work. Spending on goods and services increased. Americans wanted a fresh start. People began to move away from the cities and small towns to suburbs created out of land that had once been farmland and fields. Photographic trends were changing too. There was a new emphasis on fashion and celebrity subjects, the kind of photography Walker had always disliked. Walker was out of step with the times.

When the critic he had replaced returned from the war, *Time* magazine released Walker, but he was offered a position back at *Fortune,* also a Time-Life publication. He became the special photography editor, suggesting ideas for photo essays. Walker would remain at *Fortune* for twenty years.

Why would a person who always followed his own mind remain at a business magazine for so many years? Perhaps he was simply tired of not having money. Although the pay was modest, it was steady. Walker could now indulge his fondness for expensive Brooks Brothers clothes and fancy English shoes. And more than one friend recalled how even when short of money, Walker was ready with some cash for a friend in need.

Jane thought the job at *Fortune* was not good for Walker, that it lacked artistic challenges. He had a different point of view. "I had to use my wits there. And I think I did all right. I think I won in the long run. I was very pleased with that because that's a hard place to

Walker Evans in the 1950s

win from. That's a deadly place, really, and ghastly. . . . [I]ts values are a hundred percent the opposite of what any aesthetic or idealistic mind can ever conceive."

Walker made the most of the job. An assistant art director recalled that "Walker'd go out to photograph for two months' time, and he'd never show up at the office. . . . And one day he would trundle in and would try to sell the story he had gone out to do. Very often he would succeed."

Walker was still able to photograph subjects that had always interested him. He set up his camera at street corners in Chicago and Detroit to snap "anonymous portraits."
Click.

Two women walking down Randolph Street in Chicago. Perhaps they have just finished shopping. Perhaps they have just gotten out of work in one of the many offices in the Loop, the central business district. Are they thinking of what they have just bought? Or what they will buy? Or how they would pay their bills?

Chicago pedestrians

South side, Chicago, Illinois

He also continued to take pictures of American architecture, much of which was disappearing.

Click.

While in Chicago for *Fortune,* Walker found stately homes from an earlier generation sharing the neighborhood with newer factories.

In fact his interest during this time can be summed up in the titles of some of his photo essays: "Before They Disappear," on freight-train lettering; "The Wreckers," with photos of partially demolished old hotels, their interiors spilling out into the street to be trucked away; "Downtown: A Last Look Backward," about the destruction of older buildings in Lower Manhattan. Walker was fascinated with discarded things, not only lovely buildings but the odds and ends carelessly tossed in the gutter.

Walker may have been working for a publication that celebrated the status quo, but he maintained his stance as an outsider. "I've . . . been told . . . that my work doesn't look like establishment work, and I don't believe it does." Young photographers working in the 1950s and '60s knew and admired *American Photographs.* And Walker was always more than happy to offer advice and support. Walker met the Swiss photographer Robert Frank around 1953 and helped him receive Guggenheim awards in 1955 and 1956. Frank's work from those years was published as *The Americans,* the moody photo

Galax, Virginia, by Lee Friedlander

essay that quickly became a classic. The young American photographer Lee Friedlander sought Walker out and the two became friends. Friedlander's often witty photographs of America in the sixties earned him praise and also a Guggenheim.

The excitement of seeing young people working in a documentary style and the stability of a steady job were not enough to satisfy Walker. And he and Jane were not getting along. He would leave her to go on long assignments for *Fortune,* and when in the city, he often went to social engagements without her. Jane recalled later that she was lonely during the early fifties. In 1955 they divorced. Walker continued his job at *Fortune* and his round of socializing, going to concerts, the opera, movies, and dinners given by friends, but he seemed to be adrift. In 1959 he met a young Swiss textile designer, Isabelle Boeschenstein. Although she was married, they spent much time together. Walker showed her parts of New York that he had explored years earlier as a young man. Isabelle fell in love with Walker. She divorced her husband and asked Walker to marry her, and in October 1960 they were wed.

7

"The Street Is My Museum"

1965–1975

"You don't want your work to spring from art; you want it to commence from life, and that's the street."

At sixty-two, yet another new period began in Walker Evans's life. In 1964 he had given a talk at Yale University about his passionate interest in collecting old postcards. The auditorium was filled with enthusiastic students and teachers. The head of the graphic design department thought that Walker would make a good teacher, and after many phone messages left at *Fortune,* he convinced Walker to teach at Yale full-time. Walker retired from the magazine and left for Yale. He was not certain if he would succeed as a teacher and he certainly did not want to give formal classes. "You've been lectured at enough," he told one group of students. Rather, he would look at their photographs and share his thoughts and advice. But he would also talk with his students about movies, books, and music—everything. He discovered that he loved being around young people, and loved teaching.

In 1973 Walker bought a Polaroid SX-70 camera that made instant color pictures. When Polaroid found out that such a famous photographer was using its product, they provided him with free film—which he used with gusto. He took over two thousand SX-70 pictures in these last years, shooting with his students in the small towns and back

Walker Evans, 1974

roads of Cape Cod, Massachusetts, the eastern seaboard of Virginia, and Connecticut. He took pictures in the run-down areas close to Yale University in New Haven and on his vacation trips to England and the Caribbean island of Saint Martin.

He began reexploring subjects that had always interested him but were not appropriate for *Fortune.* Walker used the SX-70 to photograph letters and symbols on signs, buildings, and on the street pavement. He said of the lettering, "There are infinite possibilities ... as popular art, as folk art, and also as symbolism and meaning and surprise and double meaning."

Buzz. Whirr.

He went back to the gutter and the trash bin with his camera. A garbage can, occasionally can be beautiful, he wrote. In fact Walker had been a longtime collector of weathered metal roadside signs and old advertising posters, not to mention rusty discarded objects—even old pull tabs from cans. He loved these things and began to make collages with them.

Lettering

Walker made many portraits of his friends, those he had known for years and the new young friends he had made while teaching.

Rusty car

And he loved taking Polaroids of old buildings.
Buzz — Whirr.

Train station, Connecticut

Walker's health had not been good for some time. He had surgery for ulcers in 1958 and in 1972 had another serious operation on his stomach. The recovery was slow and painful. By 1974 he was so weak that at times he could barely carry even the small SX-70

58

camera. Since he was in his fifties Walker also had a serious alcohol problem. He had stopped for a while, but by 1974 he was back to drinking. His marriage to Isabelle deteriorated, and they divorced in the early '70s. Through all the poor health and personal difficulties, Walker continued to use his SX-70. The results were a wonderful late flowering of his artistry.

And he continued to give talks to students. He went to Boston on April 8, 1975, to talk to a group of Radcliffe and Harvard students. He returned to his home in Old Lyme the next day and late that night suffered a stroke. Walker Evans III died on April 10, 1975, at the age of seventy-two.

In his obituary, the art critic for the *New York Times* called Walker "one of the greatest artists of his generation." He had received recognition in museum shows, books, and critical essays. As a young man Walker learned that art could be derived from understanding and observing the society around oneself. Stare. Pry. Die knowing something—and he did. Evans's photographs are lyrical documents of his America. At times full of wit, sometimes biting and satiric, often just plain beautiful, they are his gift to us all.

Railroad sign

Notes and Quotation Sources

The following abbreviations are used in the notes and quotation sources:

AAA	*Archives of American Art*
AA	*Art in America*
BR	Belinda Rathbone
FM	*Let Us Now Praise Famous Men*
JRM	James R. Mellows
JT	Jerry Thompson
MM	Milton Meltzer
VA	*Visiting Artist*
WEW	*Walker Evans at Work*
WS	William Stott

Prologue: *A Couple at Coney Island, New York City 1928*

page

7 "I was photographing against": Cummings interview, *AAA*

1. *A Child of the Midwest, 1903−1922*

9 "I'm really spiritually at home": *VA*, pp. 317−18.

9 Instead, he entered: Rathbone, pp. 2−4.

10 "very restricted": Cummings interview, *AAA*.

10 "[S]he was great": Cummings interview, *AAA*.

10 "Fine photography is literature": *VA*, p. 313.

11 "I had a hard time": Cummings interview, *AAA*.

11 Walker changed schools several times: BR, pp. 11−22; Cummings interview, *AAA*.

2. *New York−Paris−New York, 1923−1928*

12 "I had a passion for": Cummings interview, *AAA*.

12 "I was drawn to it": Cummings interview, *AAA*.

13 Between classes: Cummings interview, *AAA;* translations in *Unclassified*, pp. 27−37.

14 "I was scared to death": Cummings interview, *AAA*.

14 "I remember my first experience": *WEW*, p. 161.

14 His real interest: Cummings interview, *AAA*.

15 "I knew I was getting educated": Cummings interview, *AAA*.

16 "He invaded you": *AA*, p. 83.

3. *Collecting Images, 1929−1935*

19 "The secret of photography": *AA*, p. 82.

19 When the light was right: *AA*, p. 84.

19 But he wondered: Cummings interview, *AAA*, p. 41.

22 "I am going to publish": letter in *Unclassified*, p. 147.

22 "After all, my father was in advertising": Cummings interview, *AAA*.

22 Lincoln recalled: *WEW*, p. 50.

24 He found that being: letters in *Unclassified*, pp. 158−165.

24 "too painful and infuriating to look at": JRM, p. 154.

24 In fact, he didn't even read: *WEW*, p. 82.

30 "to develop my own eye": Cummings interview, *AAA*.

30 "is pure record not propaganda": *WEW*, p. 112.

4. *Three Tenant Families, 1936*

35 "I don't think an artist": WS, p. 320.

35 At twenty-seven, tall, gangly: *FM*, pp. ix−x.

36 Walker was excited by the offer: *VA*, p. 318.

36 Farmers had been among: MM, pp. 92−102.

39 "Frank Ricketts? Why that": *FM*, p. 75.

39 James stayed on: BR, p. 132.

43 "pessimistic": BR, pp. 334−35.

5. *Recognition, 1937−1941*

45 "It's as though": *AA*, p. 87.

45 "I would ignore": Cummings interview, *AAA*.

46 "as documentary evidence": JRM, p. 378.

46 "a parade of dreary": BR, p. 164.

46 He wanted to photograph: *VA*, p. 317.

46 "That's my idea of what a portrait": Cummings interview, *AAA*, p. 37.

47 Among the subway riders: draft text of introduction by Evans of proposed volume of subway portraits, *WEW*, p. 160.

48 "With this hair": JRM, p. 418.

48 His Guggenheim did pay off: Cummings interview, *AAA*.

48 "There was never a better argument for": JRM, p. 446.

48 "the most realistic": JRM, p. 447.

49   *Let Us Now . . .* still read: See, for example, David Denby, "A Famous Man," *The New Yorker,* January 9, 2006, pp. 82–87, his review of Agee's collection in The Library of America series of major American writers.

6. *Fortune? 1942–1964*

50   "With a camera": *AA,* p. 29.

50   "Evans is too difficult": Cummings interview, *AAA.*

50   But it was good to have: Cummings interview, *AAA.*

51   There was a new emphasis: Cummings interview, *AAA.*

51   Jane thought: BR, p. 211.

51   "I had to use my wits": Cummings interview, *AAA.*

52   "Walker'd go out": JRM, p. 526.

54   Walker was fascinated with: *AA,* p. 85.

54   "I've been told that": *VA,* p. 312.

55   Jane recalled later that: JRM, pp. 530–548.

7. *"The Street Is My Museum," 1965–1975*

56   "the street is": *VA,* p. 314.

56   "You don't": *AA,* p. 88.

56   "You've been lectured at": *VA,* p. 311.

57   "There are infinite": Cummings interview, *AAA.*

57   A garbage can: Yale alumni magazine article *WEW,* p. 220.

57   In fact Walker was: *VA,* p. 317; also in JT, pp. 61–69.

58   By 1974, he was so weak: JT, p. 116.

59   "one of the greatest": BR, p. 307.

59   "Stare": draft text of proposed volume of subway portraits, *WEW,* p. 161.

Bibliography

The thoughts and opinions of Walker Evans are found in interviews he gave late in his life.

Oral History interview with Walker Evans conducted by Paul Cummings, 1971, *Archives of American Art / Smithsonian Institution.*

"Walker Evans, Visiting Artist: A Transcript of his Discussion with the Students of the University of Michigan," October 29, 1971, in Beaumont Newhall, ed., *Photography: Essays and Images.* (New York: Museum of Modern Art, 1980), pp. 310–20.

"Interview with Walker Evans," in *Art in America* (March–April, 1971): pp. 82–89.

I have also relied on the following excellent biographies and archival materials:

Mellow, James R. *Walker Evans.* New York: Basic Books, 1999.

Rathbone, Belinda. *Walker Evans: A Biography.* New York: Houghton Mifflin Company, 1995.

Thompson, Jerry L. *The Last Years of Walker Evans.* London: Thames and Hudson, 1997.

Rosenheim, Jeff L. and Douglas Eklund. *Unclassified: A Walker Evans Anthology.* Zurich: Scalo/New York: Metropolitan Museum of Art, 2000.

Walker Evans at Work (with an essay by Jerry L. Thompson). New York: Harper & Row, Publishers, Inc., 1982.

Many books of Walker Evans photographs have been published. These are his major publications.

American Photographs. New York: Museum of Modern Art, 1938.

Many Are Called. New Haven: Yale University Press, 2004.

Walker Evans. New York: Metropolitan Museum of Art, 2000.

Let Us Now Praise Famous Men. Boston: Houghton Mifflin Company, 1941.

General References

Meltzer, Milton. *Brother, Can You Spare a Dime? The Great Depression, 1929–33.* New York: Facts on File, 1991.

Eugène Atget (with an essay by Ben Lifson). New York: Aperture, 1997.

Stott, William. *Documentary Expressions and Thirties America.* New York: Oxford University Press, 1973.

Watkins, T. H. *The Hungry Years: A Narrative History of the Great Depression in America.* New York: Henry Holt and Company, 1999.

Chronology

1903	Born in St. Louis, Missouri.
1908	Family moves to Kenilworth, Illinois.
1914	Family moves to Toledo, Ohio.
1922	Attends Williams College. Leaves in 1923.
1924	Works in the map room of the New York Public Library. Begins to write short stories.
1926	Leaves New York for France.
1927	Returns to the United States.
1928	Moves to Brooklyn Heights.
1930	Brooklyn Bridge pictures appear in Hart Crane's poem *The Bridge.*—Photographs appear in the magazines *Hound & Horn, Creative Architecture,* and other small magazines.
1931	Photographs Victorian houses for a project by Lincoln Kirstein and John Wheelwright.
1932	Photographs appear at the Brooklyn Museum and the Albright Gallery Museum.
1933	Photographs Cuba for the book *The Crime of Cuba.*—Photographs of architecture from the Kirstein/Wheelwright project appear at the Museum of Modern Art.
1934	Commissioned for a book on architecture of the

	South and New Orleans. Meets Jane Smith Ninas in New Orleans.
1935	Appointed assistant specialist in information for the Resettlement Administration.
1936	Assigned with the writer James Agee for a *Fortune* article on white tenant farmers in the South.
1937	Loses his appointment at the Resettlement Administration.
1938	First one-person photography show at Museum of Modern Art. The book *American Photographs* is published with the exhibition.
1938	Begins subway portraits series.
1939	Jane moves to New York.
1941	Wins a Guggenheim Foundation fellowship.
1941	*Let Us Now Praise Famous Men* is published.
1941	Marries Jane.
1941	Photographs Florida for the book *The Mangrove Coast.*
1942	Hired by *Time* magazine as movie and art critic.
1945	Becomes the photography editor for *Fortune.*
1947	Retrospective at the Art Institute of Chicago.
1956	Jane leaves.
1959	Wins Second Guggenheim Foundation fellowship.
1960	Marries Isabelle Boeschenstein.
1965	Hired to teach photography at Yale University.
1966	Subway portraits are published as *Many Are Called.*
1966	Small retrospective of work is shown at the Schoelkopf Gallery, New York.
1968	Awarded an honorary doctorate of letters from Williams College.
1971	Second major retrospective, at the Museum of Modern Art, New York.
1974	Receives the National Institute of Arts and Letters Award for Distinguished Service to the Arts.
1975	Dies on April 10 after returning from a lecture in Boston.
2000	Third major retrospective, at the Metropolitan Museum of Art, New York.

Index

To Janet, with love

Acknowledgments

Thanks to Neal Porter for his editorial guidance and enthusiasm for the project; to George Wen for copyediting and moral support; to Jacklyn Burns of the J. Paul Getty Museum; Julie Zeftel, Jeff Rosenheim and Robie Rogge at the Metropolitan Museum of Art, New York City; Dan Cheek of the Fraenkel Gallery and all of the kind people at the Library of Congress for helping me obtain photographs. Thanks to Jennifer Van Dalsen for last-minute suggestions and impeccable production work. Finally, thanks to my wife Janet Pedersen, whose creativity is an inspiration and whose lovely design and suggestions have made this a better book.

All Walker Evans photographs except those taken for the United States Resettlement Administration (RA) are copyright Walker Evans Archive, The Metropolitan Museum of Art. Photographs appearing on the following pages are from the institutions listed. 2: The Metropolitan Museum of Art, Gift of Elisabeth Sekaer Rothschild and Christina Sekaer, 1994 (1994.305.1); 4: The Library of Congress (RA); 6: The Metropolitan Museum of Art, Ford Motor Company Collection, Gift of the Ford Motor Company and John C. Waddell, 1987 (1987.1100.110); 8: The Metropolitan Museum of Art, Walker Evans Archive, 1994 (1994.251.236); 10: The Metropolitan Museum of Art, Purchase, The Horace W. Goldsmith Foundation Gift, 1996 (1996.166.11); 13: The Metropolitan Museum of Art, Walker Evans Archive, 1994 (1994.255.7); 15 (left): The Metropolitan Museum of Art, Walker Evans Archive, 1994 (1994.255.75); 15 (right): The Library of Congress; 16 (top): The Metropolitan Museum of Art, Purchase, The Horace W. Goldsmith Foundation Gift, 1997 (1997.10); 16 (bottom): The Metropolitan Museum of Art, Ford Motor Company Collection, Gift of the Ford Motor Company and John C. Waddell, 1987 (1987.1100.71); 17: The Library of Congress; 18: The Metropolitan Museum of Art, Gift of Arnold H. Crane, 1972 (1972.742.3); 20 (top): The Metropolitan Museum of Art, Ford Motor Company Collection, Gift of the Ford Motor Company and John C. Waddell, 1987 (1987.1100.68); 20 (bottom): The Metropolitan Museum of Art, Walker Evans Archive, 1994 (1994.251.283); 21: The Library of Congress; 22: The Metropolitan Museum of Art, Gift of Elisabeth Sekaer Rothschild and Christina Sekaer, 1994 (1994.305.1); 23: The Library of Congress; 25, 26: The J. Paul Getty Museum; 27: The Library of Congress (RA); 28: The Metropolitan Museum of Art, Walker Evans Archive, 1994 (1994.441.34); 29, 30: The Library of Congress; 31, 32, 33, 34: The Library of Congress (RA); 37: The Metropolitan Museum of Art, Walker Evans Archive, 1994 (1994.254.11); 38, 40, 41, 42, 43, 44: The Library of Congress (RA); 47 (top): The J. Paul Getty Museum; 47 (bottom): The Metropolitan Museum of Art, Walker Evans Archive, 1994 (1994.253.514.1); 49: The J. Paul Getty Musuem; 51: The Metropolitan Museum of Art, Walker Evans Archive, 1994 (1994.261.72); 52: The Metropolitan Museum of Art, Purchase, The Horace W. Goldsmith Foundation Gift, 1990 (1990.1045); 53: The J. Paul Getty Museum; 54: courtesy of the Fraenkel Gallery, San Francisco; 57 (top): The Metropolitan Museum of Art, Gift of the artist, 1996 (1996.206.25); 57 (bottom): The Metropolitan Museum of Art, Purchase, Samuel J. Wagstaff Jr. Bequest and Lila Acheson Wallace Gift, 1994 (1994.245.30); 58 (top): The Metropolitan Museum of Art, Purchase, Samuel J. Wagstaff Jr. Bequest and Lila Acheson Wallace Gift, 1994 (1994.245.74); 58: (bottom): The Metropolitan Museum of Art, Purchase, Samuel J. Wagstaff Jr. Bequest and Lila Acheson Wallace Gift, 1994 (1994.245.124); 59: The Metropolitan Museum of Art, Purchase, Samuel J. Wagstaff Jr. Bequest and Lila Acheson Wallace Gift, 1994 (1994.245.44).

Distributed in Canada by H. B. Fenn and Company, Ltd.

Library of Congress Cataloging-in-Publication Data

Nau, Thomas.
Walker Evans: Photographer of America / Thomas Nau.
p. cm.
Includes bibliographical references.
ISBN-13: 978-1-59643-225-3
ISBN-10: 1-59643-225-X
1. Evans, Walker, 1903-1975—Juvenile literature. 2. Photographers—United States—Biography—Juvenile literature. I. Title.
TR140.E92N38 2007
770.92—dc22
[B]
2006012900

Roaring Brook Press books are available for special promotions and premiums.
For details, contact: Director of Special Markets, Holtzbrinck Publishers.

Book design by Janet Pedersen

Printed in China on acid-free paper.

First edition April 2007

1 3 5 7 9 10 8 6 4 2